T0065363

Strength in the Darkness

Islande Schettini

authorHOUSE®

AuthorHouse™
1663 Liberty Drive
Bloomington, IN 47403
www.authorhouse.com
Phone: 833-262-8899

Published by AuthorHouse 01/29/2021

ISBN: 978-1-6655-1558-0 (sc)
ISBN: 978-1-6655-1557-3 (e)

Library of Congress Control Number: 2021901896

Print information available on the last page.

Any people depicted in stock imagery provided by Getty Images are models, and such images are being used for illustrative purposes only. Certain stock imagery © Getty Images.

This book is printed on acid-free paper.

To my children,
Royce, Renald Jr., and Isaac:
You are my biggest inspiration. I am glad I got to be
your mama in this life,and I love you all.

My mom: Jeannine Edouarzin
My brother: Marc-Arthur Souis

Editor, counselor : Pastor Sony Joseph
My cousin Fritzner Sterlin, Katia Bolivard, Johnson Edouarzin

Supporters and friends:
Nathacha Pierre Louis
Robinson Valvert
Guito Laguerre
Arline Louis
Emmanuela Andre
Josue Vulmenay

So do not fear, for I am with you; do not be
dismayed, for I am your God.
—Isaiah 41:10 (NIV)

Contents

Strength in the Darkness

*In the darkness, Jesus helped me see the light. Through Him,
I found peace. That is one of the reasons I love Him so much:
He is my strength in the darkness.*

Her smile helps the sun shine.
Bright everywhere she goes.
Been through tough times.
As a rock, she stays strong.
"Black don't crack," they say.
She has been through hell growing up:
Thirteen was dark. She cried.
It takes courage to live it all.

Life was sharp like a knife,
Tastes sour like a vinegar.
Things got hard and harder,
But she decided to shine.

When things were bad, she never gave up;
Instead, she flourished,
Blooming like a petaled rose,
Bright like a star,
While staying strong.

She believes
Everything happens for a reason.
She embraced life, sought God.
She got her strength from the darkness.

My Master Perfect Love

Knowing God is the key that brings happiness. Knowing how much Jesus loves us makes us embrace life more fully. We are serving a Master who loves us unconditionally. He proved that by sending Jesus so we can be saved.

Through danger, you carry me away,
Hide me deep inside a grid.
You show me love along the way.
You are the perfect aid.

When trouble comes, you give me courage.
Under your wings, I feel like a superstar.
Even in my sleep, I found hope.
Your grace is spectacular.

I am no longer a slave to fear.
You gave yourself in sacrifice so I can reign.
Now I am able to fight like a polar bear.
Free to follow You till the end, with no pain

My Father Lives in Heaven

And do not call anyone on earth 'father,' for you
have one Father, and he is in heaven.
—Matthew 23:9 (NIV)

The Lord is my Father; I do not miss a thing.
He provides for me; I do not need anything.
Even when I cannot see Him, I know He is nearby.
In my need, He provides and acts!

I am grateful for His love every day.
He lifts my chin when it faces down;
Always put me together after a meltdown.
I do not know what I would do without His love.

At the cross, Christ gave it all.
To save and make me a Royal Priest.
I was bought at a big price.
Now I am living with no tears.

I am waiting for the day to come—
The day I will finally meet Him.
All fights, the race, will be done.
Even the earth will be redone.

The Lord is my Father; I do not need a thing.
Try to put me down, it will not change anything.
I have hope and trust from above.
Cannot play! I must keep my head high.

About you—what are you waiting for?
You are the one Jesus is waiting for.
Hurry! There is not much time.
If you read this, today is the perfect day.

Stay, Candor

We are called to be different. Seek what you are here for and fight to achieve it. Life is a battle. Do not let anything keep you from your destination.

Be your own light; your future is bright.
Shine on your own time.
Do not let anyone hold you too tight.
Try not to get involved in any crime.
Don't be despair in the middle of the night:
Open your wings to fly when it's time.
Enjoy your time—do not let lowlife!
Affect your pride like broadcast.
Be bold: it is not the end of life.
Stop thinking about the past!
Follow your heart; do not go back.
Love yourself and stay candor.
Do not be afraid to shine in the dark,
Bright like a projector, brave as a warrior.

The Meaning of Love

Love is patient, love is kind. It does not envy, it does not boast, it is not proud. It is not rude, it is not self-seeking, it is not easily angered, it keeps no record of wrongs.
—1 Corinthians 13:1 (NIV)

Love is not fake but genuine.

Love never loses—win!
Love is not weak but tenacious.
Love is not a coward but a hero.
Love is not pushy but gentle.
Love does not hate; pleasant.
Love is not ugly.
Beautiful love does not retain, it shares.
Love does not discourage, it persuades.
Love is not careless but attentive.
Love saves, it does not endanger.

A Wife Is a Crystal

He who finds a wife finds a good thing and obtains favor from the Lord.
—Proverbs 18:22 (NKJV)

Color her with your love,
Make people value her.
As a marble, she should be polished.
Like a crystal, let her shine.
A wife is precious:
She is a diamond.
A good wife is a treasure.
Take good care of her—
She is your crystal forever.

The Right One

On the road, you will meet people. You will sometimes meet the wrong one, but do not rush—wait on God, because the right one does exist. The person will come when you least expect it. Just believe: nothing is impossible.

When you meet the right one,
You will know.
It is different,
Reassuring.

When you meet the right one,
You will know.
It is passionate,
You won't feel scared.

When you met the right one,
You will know.
It is natural.
It will bring happiness.

When you meet the right one,
You will know.
There is no stress,
You will gleam.

When you finally meet the one,
You will know.
It will feel great—
Believe it! You will see.

I Met You at the Right Time

There are moments to feel down thinking that everything is over, but let me tell you, life is not over for you yet. There is hope. There is always hope for whoever believes.

My life was empty—could not let go of the past;
Suffering inside—I wanted time to go fast.
I didn't trust anyone; I was living like a ghost.
I was worried, afraid I would be toast.

Insecure, I didn't know my worth.
I was desperate—couldn't bear my thoughts—
Until I met you. Everything makes sense now.
You promise to love me forever—wow!

You taught me patience and kindness. Up there
I knew that my strength came from somewhere,
But I could not believe that I was changing.
Every day I was struggling to make a living.

You came along to save me.
At my lowest point, you came to deliver me.
Step by step, I am forgetting yesterday.
I trust that every day, you will make a way.

More than ever now, I want to win the race.
Full of strength—it is not a coincidence.
You came on time to help me fight.
My Savior: You are my biggest light.

On the Side of the Road

For anyone who is facing a difficult time.

It might be a boyfriend or a husband who left you on the side of the road. You must know that most of the time things happen in our lives for a reason, and we need to learn from them. Challenges are here to strengthen us. We must face them to become successful.

Walking on the side of the road,
You will meet people, but they will not stay aboard.
Life is a boat—do not get attached to the wrong cord.
Let it go! Trust the Lord.

Pickups on the road can give regret.
Nabals will talk like trumpets.
With no truth. They play croquet.
Believe! You will be ridden like a jet.

Life is a boat—choose who comes inside.
Let no one do you like horsehide.
Protect your heart from people outside.
Look up high; don't be on the blind side.

They are mindblowers:
They will drive you like helicopters.

Sad Ending: A Love Forever

Life doesn't come the way we expect it to. Sometimes we meet the right people at the wrong time. As life goes, you will forget and move on.

They met one Sunday morning at church,
became inseparable and best friends.

Both kept the relationship spiritual, until

One day he got an offer to leave town, follow his dream as an actor.
Hope was to see each other again,
But on the way he got lost in the fame, forgot
home, forgot his best friend.

The only choice is watching him on TV,

Making love to these beautiful women. She felt discouraged.
Hoping to tell him the truth one day,

She is praying for the dream to come true,
The dream of marrying her best friend. It is a fantasy.

Her secret is safe within her, though.

No one knows why she cannot move on,
But she gave her heart years ago.

To someone who does not even know. The phone rings!
She finally has him to win.

She is trying to explain the reason behind it—

A voice in the background …
She was not invited.

Nothing to do about it; she will never forgive him.
After nine years, finally back where it started,
He found a letter on the table (*whatsoever*):

She was tired of waiting forever.
Crying his way out, he felt unlucky that she
did not know how he felt all along:

He was waiting for her, didn't want to ruin the friendship.

All that time … she will never know this love was meant to be hers.

Past Melancholy

I had a hard time trusting others because of past relationships. I did not believe in myself—I felt hopeless. I encourage everyone to trust God. Let Him guide you, and you will find your way out.

Life is not the same anymore
Dark in my heart,
Hard to let go of the past.
It's bothering me because.
I know how you feel about me,
But, baby, please forgive me.
I hope you understand.
Where I stand.
I am with you even though it seems otherwise—
I care for you.
Deeply, in a way
You cannot imagine,
But I feel selfish, not able to trust.
Nor accept that someone can love me.
For *me*.
I am raging inside, but God is working on me.
I know He will fix me.
I mean, if He can send you,
Let us trust Him.
Please hold my hands,
Be ready to face bad moments.
I promise to love you the way you deserve.
We all want the same things.
You and I got hurt the same way.
Believe me, it is hard to let go.
I am still hanging there,
Behind my thinking—

Islande Schettini

Hard to move on after all.
But I can do this if you hold me tight.
Even when I ask you to leave,
Do not accept my fight!
You are my light.
If you agree,
I am willing to change.
It is not impossible to carry on—
We both deserve a great future,
A future that I look forward to.
If you hold my hands, Boo,
I will forget this past melancholy.

Burden

I feel like crying,

                         Nothing feels right.
                           I keep going back

Every time
To the bad guy.
Inside of me, hurt.
I feel nuts
To trust,

                         But I feel so lonely.

            How can I survive this agony?

My bed is empty
At night.

                    Ready! But where is he?
                    Here, but do not feel it.
            I am just a body without a soul.

My heart is heavy, I feel crazy.

               Why such a burden?
            Ain't committed no crime.

I guess that is what I get

          For dating the wrong guy, all the time.

It's OK

Sometimes life can be hard—the Bible tells us that God is near in difficult times.

He is not only our Father, He's our protector, friend, counselor; but He's also everything for us, and He knows what we need. When we fall back down, do not stay down, get up and keep going because the victory belongs to people who believe in God.

It's OK to fall,
Get up.
It's OK to get hurt,
Start over.
It's OK to be different,
Just be yourself.
It's OK to live life,
Do the right thing.
It's OK to make mistakes,
Learn from it.
Life is a school—
On the way, you will meet people,
Does not mean they will stay.
It's OK to trust though,
To love all over again.
Don't be afraid to try the rain.

Importance of Life

During the coronavirus pandemic, I have learned the importance of health, friends, and family. We have all learned this because it is such a difficult time for all of us. I have promised myself to cherish every minute of my life from now on.

Health is precious when we are sick.
Time is important when we are late.
People are missing when they are gone.
Want to go outside, but we cannot.
We take for granted our lives, until we lost it.
Made excuses not to go to work, now we need it.
Want to give anything to be with our friends,
But we used to be too busy to see them.
Always lazy to go to church, but now we need prayer.
We hope for a change after this virus goes.
We must make a change to love more, enjoying life like a Pro.
Knowing that we only have each other,
I and you were created to live together.

Health is important.
Time is special.
Family is needed.
Friends are the best.
Prayer is the key.
Work to survive.
Life is important.

Disaster Bomb

Seventy years ago, the Hiroshima atomic bomb killed nearly 80,000 people. Some of these people were kids who will never see a future because of this monster. We say "no" today to destruction, racism—we want our kids to have a better future, a free will.

Catastrophe, boom!
What is going on?
Bomb! People are running on the street everywhere,
Suspect on the run; police cannot catch up to save the world.
Jail he faces for killing innocent human beings.
Why so much hate? So many crimes
On what we are supposed to call a paradise,
Created for us to fill with love and peace.
What happens, are we giving up on finding peace?
While countries chasing their dreams, we cannot even move on.
Frustration! Can't even get out for fun; do not believe anymore in paradise.
Bombers sit in jail; innocent lay in tombs everywhere.
We need to do something about destructive substance unless we stop un-being.
Stop building them, or we going to make more people cry in the world.
Watching movies gives pleasure, but it is poison for the world.
Our kids feel like living in a monster spot—can't enjoy lullaby in peace.
All they do is learn on YouTube. They don't behave like a human being.
Single parents struggle to instruct kids about what to put on
Because police gunshot is everywhere.
Supposed to go after bad boy, not innocent in paradise.

Catastrophe change, mistrust, tantrum arrive in this world.
We are scared for our kids everywhere!
Dead, funeral instead of fighting for change, praying for peace.
We build catacombs, fill them with fake dreams.

Islande Schettini

We cannot be distrustful unless we stop being.
Etiquette, change as we move forward to our wellbeing.
We need to stop the booming—live again in paradise.
Forgive, forget, try to move on.
Hopeful to create another world
For our kids to finally live—in peace.
We can walk, run, talk everywhere
Without hurting each other,
Make the world a paradise.
Police! Stop been walking on.
Our innocent kids in the world,
Let them live beautifully; let us create peace.
So, boom! Boom! Gunshot can stop everywhere.

Racism Is a Disease

Being black has nothing to do with racism, it is just the way you see yourself toward other people. In 2020 we don't have time for negative vibes, it's time to love one another. Be humble, keep it simple.

Real than you can imagine,
It is a killer.
Stronger than corona,
It is a virus
That you cannot trust to be around.
Some people hide it inside—
They are cruel,
Do not stay close to them,
You can't ever know.
They will show love but fake.
It is crucial—
Racism is real even when you think it's weird.
It is a big deal when you do not feel accepted.
Black is as important as everyone,
A human being.
Racism makes you worried,
You think you unlucky.
Racism causes hate crimes,
People dying every day.
Thinking what tomorrow will bring,
Our kids' future is messed up.
Racism is a disease, a killer,
Stay away from it.

Oh, Countryside!

When I left my country to come to the U.S., it was hard. I had to leave my friends and family behind. The worst part of all was I had to start over with new jobs, school. Still, now I miss Haiti—one day I will go back to see my family.

Missing the birds,
Missing the horses,
Morning and night,
When the breeze hit me, wondering why I am here!
Missing home,
Missing friends,
Where good relations stand.
People care about each other,
Family member still visits;
TV does not replace books.
Missing sunshine,
Kids still playing outside.
America is a dream come true,
But I miss warm weather in December.
Missing *fritay* at night.
Oh, sweet home! I miss you.
I miss my first love,
In summer, at the park.
Missing all the fun.
America! No time,
Focus is on the bills.
Missing home too much.
I am praying one day
To go back,
After the kids make a living,
Make a life,
With a smile, hopefully,
To return *au bercail*.

What a Coincidence

To be alive in 2010 after the 7.1 earthquake in Haiti, you must know that God has a plan for you. That day I was sleeping *but* thank God someone woke me up. I am alive today because my mission was not done. I will never forget about how many people died on the street, I will carry the pain for friends, close family, and everyone else who died that day.

You just wake up one day,
Wishing condolences
To people you saw yesterday.
You just wake up one day
To a desolate roof.
Kids, woman, died on the street
Without weatherproof,
To a desolate roof.
Left people with no work.
Without weatherproof,
Most of us live on a sidewalk.
Left people with no work,

Wishing condolences.
Most of us live on a sidewalk.

Peace

Mankind needs to come together to seek peace. It does not matter who you are: white, black, or yellow we all need it—Jesus is the source.

Peace be with you all.
Since the beginning, He knows about the call.
The call to plead guilty, to cover all,
But sometimes, we took it small.

Living in peace is marvelous,
Its sound is mellifluous.
Seek peace, you will be victorious
Because it is precious.

Rich, poor, we all need it,
Everywhere are fighting for it.

Peace does not show up unless you seek for it
Through Jesus Christ; believe, you will get it.

News

Jesus said to them, "Go into all the world and
preach the gospel to all creation."
—Mark 16:15 (NIV)

(1)
Share the news!
To our surroundings
In a heartbeat, things can be deterring
Before Jesus left, He told us to preach the Gospel
But you and I, are so busy in life, we take it personal
Never realize, our brothers and sisters, can be missing heaven
Outside of God wings, they can be squeeze, until they lost oxygen
Wake up Christians! it is our job to make sure, they will get there

(4)
Them the way
Let them know that
Jesus
Is
The
Key
To
Open doors

(2)
We have mandated
To encourage them
Help them take the
Step, to follow Jesus
Be patient with them
Like He is with us

(3)
They can get busted
Hostage by the devil
Sometimes they are
Not going to listen
But we must be
A model to show

There's Always a Sweet Voice

My sheep hear my voice, and I know them, and they follow me.
—John 10:27 (NKJV)

There is a sweet voice;
If I hear it, you can too.
Start seeking for it to gain
Cover when it rains.
This voice ensures
Help; you endure.
When bad times occur,
Give you a sense of humor.
There is a sweet voice in the air
To hold you when others leave you.
When everything is going down,
The world is turning around,
There is a sweet voice
To reassure you that things will be fine.
I hear it through the wind, you can too
If you pay attention after you pray.
There is always a sweet voice
To hear you when crying out.

Visit from Above

God's presence is everything. I remembered a song that we used to sing back in church while I was in my country (Haiti), "God's presence is more precious than gold, nothing compares to its magnificence."

Visit me tonight,
I will leave the door open
And the light.

On the mountain, meet me halfway
When I go to pray.
Visit me at night
To help me gain
Strength for my battles,
To kill the devil.
God, your visit brings me comfort
When I do not know where to go.

When you visit,
Trees are resplendent,
Hearts are melting,
Dead's reviving.
It is reassuring,
Please, visit me more often.

Aquarium

When I met Jesus, I was at my deepest level. He has the keys to all my chains. God's presence is like water to me; when I am in it, I breathe like a fish—I am a better person.

Your presence is like water,
When I feel bad, I left like a warrior,
Like a lost fish swimming wherever,
Sometimes on the way, I catch high fever.

I lost power, breathing becomes heavier.
Your presence to me is like water,
I need to go back forever,
Stay there to feel better.

Your love for me does matter
When facing challenge whatsoever.
I run away like an unbeliever,
You look for me all over.

You forgive me for whatever,
Treat me like a new customer.
For so long I was doing crossover,
Now, I decided to serve you, Master.

Empty Jar

Every Christian feels empty sometimes, we feel hopeless but always remember that Jesus is here to fill our heart when feeling down—count on it. Just let Him in, you will see change.

Jesus came to fill the empty heart;
Brokenness, sadness is part.
He will not let you break in part;
Promise to never leave us apart.

Time to let Jesus in;
For him, we aren't a pain.
We can be far away from Spain.
He will be with us in the middle of the rain.

Do not be afraid to make the path!
It is not too late—don't let the dream fade.
There is a promise wide
To help us ride.

We are not fighting in vain
Because in the end,
We will be with Him.
While the devil burns in pain,
We will rejoice in Him.

Strong, we must stay strong!
We were chosen
To serve God, for lifelong.
Hallelujah will be our song.

He's Mine

Jesus saves me now, I am victorious. I am no longer a slave because of His unconditional love. I can say that Jesus is mine and I am His forever, I am waiting for the day to go home.

I love Him, but He loves me first.
I suffered while waiting for him,
But He is here now,
And He is mine—
Mine for a lifetime.
Love is perfect with Him.
I am over with depression,
My head is clear of doubt.
I don't feel lonely anymore.
I cannot leave Him, since we met
We are perfect for each other.
I am weak, but He is strong.
He promises He will never leave me.
I am not afraid
To let go of the past.
I am not afraid to
Float, holding His hands.
It is a wonderful feeling,
A tremendous experience, I am trusting His love.
I am letting Him take over,
To bring me wherever.
When time comes,
To finally take me home.

Unforgettable Pass

I was found by those who did not seek me; I revealed
myself to those who did not ask for me.
—Roman 10:20 (NIV)

I was trouble while living in a bubble;
Enjoying my time, but I was in trouble.
I found myself caught in the muddy puddle.
My life was confused, it was unstoppable.

People tried to tell me, "No," but I was uncontrollable.
All I wanted was suicidal—I found myself eligible.
One day Christ found me—I was able to rekindle.
His love saved me—it is unforgettable.

I found my way out of the darkness;
Now I am working in His forgiveness.
I have joy, peace, clarity, no guiltiness.
I do nothing to deserve His goodness.

I know, He won't let me go back there again;
His sacrifice on the cross was not in vain.
No longer thirsty, I am drinking in his fountain.
I will glorify His name with no restraint.

Rules to Be Happy

It is true that God created us with a purpose, but we are free to choose our own path in life; we can choose to be good or bad.

You can see, do not touch.
You can eat, not too much.

You can hear, not everything.
You can talk, control your mouth.

You can walk, watch your step.
You can run, not too fast.

You can drive, no speeding.
You can die, don't die young.
You can love, protect your heart.
You can marry, chose wisely.

You can have kids, not too many.
You can share, do not give it all.

You can work, take time to enjoy life.
You can save, don't be too greedy.

You can be sad, do not cry.
You can be happy, just avoid trouble.

You can be mad, stay kind.
You can be good if you want.

You can learn, stay focus.
You can get there if you try.

Fall

I like fall, I think most of us agree on that Fall is one of the best seasons—kids are playing trick or treat outside; the trees are changing color; leaves are everywhere. Fall makes us prepare for winter. It is thanksgiving time.

Rainbows, the color of the trees;
The weather is between warm, cold.
Birds flying to make nests;
Leaves fall off the trees.
The wind blows, leaves fly.
Kids play trick or treat.
Beautiful stars in the sky;
Fall announces winter.

Black Friday is nearby;
Turkey dinner in November.
Pumpkin pie everywhere;
Stores are crowded.
Preparing for Christmas,
Students are racing for grades
To receive the best gift—
They will do anything.

Fall is beautiful;
It is time to be thankful.

Christmas Is the Best Time of the Year

My father was a big fan of Christmas, so I grew up celebrating it. My father and I used to eat chocolate kisses, drank eggnogs—it was the perfect time. After he died, I always remember him on Christmas day. It was his favorite holiday.

Best time to forgive and forget.
Best time for people to gather and celebrate.
Best time of the year to make peace, take risks,
To give without waiting for a lifted.
Best time for the snow to start falling.
Best time for kids to play the snowman.
Best time to eat, pray, and laugh—
No time for sadness, time to have fun.
Best time of the year to make peace.
Best time to make change and clean.
Best time to love yourself, love others.
It is a time for kids to greet elders.
It was the birth of Jesus—
Best time all around the world.

Mon Zaku

I called you Mon Zaku—
In the Lion King, you talk like Zazu.

> Your dad wanted a girl, not you.
> He creates a situation, callous,
> Makes life onerous.
> He thought you are not precious.

No worries, Mama got you.
She will fight for you *jusqu'au bou*.
Life would be empty without you.

> To God be the glory
> Because you are healthy,
> And you are welcome in my family.

> Your life will be extravagant.
> You are particularly important.
> Wherever you go, you are so brilliant.

> Cannot live without you,
> You are my Teddy bear.
> No worries, Mama got you.

My Pink Hat

I get used to things; doesn't mean I am a materialist. If you know me, you will know that I get attached to things like hats or a pair of jeans that I feel comfortable wearing. This poem is about a hat that I like so much, in winter I never go anywhere without it—this pink hat got my heart.

I have a pink hat
To hide sins from the heart.
Messy hair, I wear it when the sun is hot.
Cold, warm, I am perfect with my hat.

Everywhere, people got jealous because of it.
Everyone asking where I bought it.
My hat keeps me calm in bad times.
I use it when doing Facetime.

I love my pink hat for life.
When I put it on, my outfit looks highlife.
We became one until the end.
No one can break where we stand.

I even have it in my dream.
If I don't wear it, I daydream.
I will protect my pink hat with my bazooka
Until it gets famous, like a singer opera.

Oh Shadow

When I was a kid I used to play with my shadow—it was my best friend. Your shadow will always be by your side.

Why following me everywhere I go? I walk! You walk! Oh-oh!
When I run; you run bro.

It is not a joke!
You will get a poke.
I am not in the mood to play with you.
Even the sun complains about you—

When it goes left, you go right!
Why act like that?
Are you all alright?

You copy me in everything!
Why do you do such a thing?

Let us make a deal with each other!
Don't be annoying, follow my order.
When I am walking,
Stop walking.

Stop following me,
Or you will get bit up by me!
Be careful, sometimes you make me scared.
You walk too close, like a coward.

Islande Schettini

You can receive any headbutt,
Straight in the butt.
Stop imitating me!
You do not want to see the real me

You make me dance,

I do not like it.
And I am not happy about it!
You give me no choice but to fall for it.

We Are Passengers Like Birds

We are not supposed to let stress control our lives, always remember that we are passengers. One day we will go, without anything, just our body, so do not stress over things that you don't need.

A bird does not have a fixed place—when it's time, it will fly.
Birds do not stress, they have no credit card debt.
Birds do not get attached,
They know they aren't staying for long.
Birds are always happy; they do not worry.
Birds know God will provide.
They just do their part by singing in the sky,
They were created for that.
If only people lived like a bird, they'll do their part.
By providing love, peace, being kind to one another.
The world would be a better place,
A safe place to live in
Until the end.
Like birds, we are not going to stay forever,
We are travelers.

Black Don't Crack, No Matter What

Black is from Africa; we are everywhere, does not mean we are not united. When we see each other, we become family, we care for each other. The love is there; we bring hope everywhere we go. We will never crack; we will be smiling till the end.

Until then, this is going to stop,
Thinking that you better than us.
What makes you think you famous?
Were you created on planet Uranus?

You must learn to live with us
We are not going nowhere, bro.
We seek freedom long ago
To live with no cost, like a hero.

Stop killing, forcing us to hate you.
Black will not crack just to please you.
We were not born to follow you.
The trap you set up will be for you.

We know you don't like us,
Even when you pretend to die for us.
You always look suspicious.
It is hard to hide it, it is irreligious.

Being a slave for 246 years
With no pay, no gain, no rest!
We deserves at least,
To die in peace.

Loving You Left Me Poor

Past relationships can be messy when you have a bad breakup, but you need to follow your heart; do what is good for you. Never let anyone make you feel guilty about leaving them if they are not good for you.

One perfect day a gentle breeze hit my heart!
Made me believe a fairytale exists—you smart!
It was too good to be true, you stir me apart!
You go again, left me in pain.
My heart is crying in vain!
For you to see there's still rain.
How can you change things in a heartbeat?
And replace me that quick—I forbid it!
Calling me in the middle of the night to doublespeak,
It is not enough when you cheated—freak!
Wanted to come back when you needed it,
Just to make sure you finish it.
I knew you were weak,
But now you prove it.

A Letter to My Ex

"A Letter to My Ex" was inspired by a past relationship. He was my first love.

Never thought I would see you again.
One day, came across you—very strange.
That is a lie when you said you married in vain.
You decided with no voyage.
Back home, I was waiting for you,
Thinking one day you will come back.
My dream never come true because of you.
Can't do nothing—you take me aback.

You said, "Let's be friends"!
Cannot go back to change anything.
You did this to us, ex-boyfriend,
Did not come back to finish the thing.
Now you need a place to play
Because you cannot live with the pain.
Does my smile bother you? Sorry can't replay.
I prefer to keep my distance—forget the pain.
Good start but sad ending,
Cannot go back as nothing happened.
Move on, stop faking.
Leave the wounds closed, do not reopen.
I already moved on, do the same.

Your Kiss

*There are moments you can never forget—like your first kiss,
your first love. They are stored in your heart forever.*

I remember like it was yesterday,
When you kissed me for the first time,
It was my first crime.
If grandma knew, she would use you like a dime.
I dreamed of it all the time.
When that happened, I did not want it to end.
Your lips, sweet like a strawberry,
Made my lips pretty like Gucci.
I remember that time,
I wish I can turn time
To have you do it again.
Because he does not do it like you.
Your kiss will always remembered.

Let It Go

*Make people in your life feel important, embrace them. Make
them feel that you love them because it can be too late if you
let the chance pass—you do not know how long they will be
with you.*

Like the stars, love shines.
A beautiful morning when you left.
Cried alone; life was empty with the kids.
Everyone was sad but you.

Enjoying life with a new girl,
Never think about your family once.
Now you want her back to torture.
Let it go, you are not going to die.

Three kids—you should be ashamed.
Boys need the father along the way,
When beating the mother in front of them!
What did you expected?

Think twenty years from now
When stepdad gets to take your place.
You will never come to a football game,
Will never be in their birthdays.

Do not regret something you never love.
Now you remember you have a family.
Let it go, don't worry about it;
You can't even play a fake father.
When the kids become heroes
I am sure you will be there to Mingo.

Wintertime

I do not think any of us like winter, especially when it's too cold. I despise wintertime, I prefer summer.

Foot crack, dry lips freezing cold.
Snow rise, got stuck near home.
Catch cold while waiting in the cold.
Missing comfort inside my home.

Wrong time to be alone.
Wintertime, the feeling gets worse.
The best thing to have is a backbone
At night, cold feet are worse.

Leaving him in winter is not the best.
I think I am in a hot mess!
Feel worse, I have regrets—
Cold sheet, loneliness.

I must be fine, no breakdown!
Nothing can put me down,
I was born to be strong.

Growing

Growing in the love of Christ is the best way for someone to grow. You can grow in love, joy, peace, kindness, faithfulness, generosity ...

Let us grow in the love of Christ.
Do not try to do otherwise,
Let us practice love!

We do not deserve God's freedom,
But He sent his son to die for us as true love.
The plan behind it was to give us wisdom!

Through Jesus, we have eternal life for free.
Let us love, forgive others as He forgive us.
Live in peace because we are carefree!

Do not be afraid, nothing can happen to us!
We are loved; Amazing creatures
We are precious in the eyes of God.

We are a new creation.
Life is great in the Lord!
Let us grow in the love of Christ.

The End

Printed in the United States
By Bookmasters